The *C*harge of the Light Brigade and Other Poems

By Alfred Lord Tennyson

Includes MLA Style Citations for Scholarly Secondary Sources, Peer-Reviewed Journal Articles and Critical Academic Research Essays

Squid Ink Classics

The *C*harge of the Light Brigade and Other Poems

By Alfred Lord Tennyson

Includes MLA Style Citations for Scholarly Secondary Sources, Peer-Reviewed Journal Articles and Critical Academic Research Essays

Squid Ink Classics

Library of Congress Cataloging in Publication Data

Squid Ink Classics

ISBN-13:
978-1987761276

ISBN-10:
1987761278

Published by Squid Ink Classics

Boston, Massachusetts

The Charge of the Light Brigade

This poem celebrates a famous charge at Balaklava in the Crimean War, October 25, 1854. The Russian army had advanced to threaten Balaklava, the base of supplies of the allied French, English, and Turkish forces. The first attack of Russian was repelled, and at about eleven o'clock, the Light Brigade, consisting of 673 men, was ordered to charge a Russian battery a mile and a half away. The order was evidently an error, but it was obeyed with splendid gallantry and matchless bravery on the part of the British soldiers, only 195 surviving the merciless storm of shot and shell.

Tennyson got the suggestion for this poem in the report of the War Correspondent of the London Times, printed November 14, 1854, and in the editorial published the day before. The editorial is in part as follows:

"The whole brigade advanced at a trot for more than

a mile, down a valley, with a murderous flank fire of

Minie muskets and shells from the hills on both sides.

It charged batteries, took guns, sabered the gunners,

and charged the Russian cavalry beyond; but, being

attacked by cavalry in front and rear, it had to cut its

way through them, and return through the same cavalry

and the same fire. The British soldier will do his duty, even to certain death, and is not paralyzed by feeling that he is the victim of some hideous blunder. Splendid as the event was on the Alma (brilliant Russian defeat in the same campaign in September) yet that rugged ascent was scarcely so glorious as the progress of the cavalry through and through that valley of death, with a murderous fire, not only in front, but on both sides, above, and even in the rear."

Tennyson wrote this poem in a few minutes on December 2, 1854. In August of the following year, hearing that the soldiers before Sebastopol were enthusiastic over his war poem, he had a thousand copies printed on separate quarto sheets, and sent them out to the soldiers of the Crimea with his compliments, for he wanted them, as he said in a note printed with the poem, "to know that those who sit at home love and honor them."

From: Searson, James William, and George Ellsworth Martin. *Studies in Reading*. Vol. 5. University Publishing Company, 1912.

The Charge of the Light Brigade

I

Half a league, half a league,

Half a league onward,

All in the valley of Death

  Rode the six hundred.

"Forward, the Light Brigade!

Charge for the guns!" he said.

Into the valley of Death

  Rode the six hundred.

II

"Forward, the Light Brigade!"

Was there a man dismayed?

Not though the soldier knew

  Someone had blundered.

Theirs not to make reply,

Theirs not to reason why,

Theirs but to do and die.

Into the valley of Death

Rode the six hundred.

III

Cannon to right of them,

Cannon to left of them,

Cannon in front of them

   Volleyed and thundered;

Stormed at with shot and shell,

Boldly they rode and well,

Into the jaws of Death,

Into the mouth of hell

   Rode the six hundred.

IV

Flashed all their sabres bare,

Flashed as they turned in air

Sabring the gunners there,

Charging an army, while

   All the world wondered.

Plunged in the battery-smoke

Right through the line they broke;

Cossack and Russian

Reeled from the sabre stroke

   Shattered and sundered.

Then they rode back, but not

   Not the six hundred.

V

Cannon to right of them,

Cannon to left of them,

Cannon behind them

   Volleyed and thundered;

Stormed at with shot and shell,

While horse and hero fell.

They that had fought so well

Came through the jaws of Death,

Back from the mouth of hell,

All that was left of them,

   Left of six hundred.

VI

When can their glory fade?

O the wild charge they made!

  All the world wondered.

Honour the charge they made!

Honour the Light Brigade,

   Noble six hundred!

Break, Break, Break

Break, break, break,

    On thy cold gray stones, O Sea!

And I would that my tongue could utter

    The thoughts that arise in me.

O, well for the fisherman's boy,

    That he shouts with his sister at play!

O, well for the sailor lad,

    That he sings in his boat on the bay!

And the stately ships go on

    To their haven under the hill;

But O for the touch of a vanish'd hand,

    And the sound of a voice that is still!

Break, break, break

    At the foot of thy crags, O Sea!

But the tender grace of a day that is dead

Will never come back to me.

Claribel

Where Claribel low-lieth
The breezes pause and die,
Letting the rose-leaves fall:
But the solemn oak-tree sigheth,
Thick-leaved, ambrosial,
With an ancient melody
Of an inward agony,
Where Claribel low-lieth.

At eve the beetle boometh
Athwart the thicket lone:
At noon the wild bee hummeth
About the moss'd headstone:
At midnight the moon cometh,
And looketh down alone.
Her song the lintwhite swelleth,
The clear-voiced mavis dwelleth,
The callow throstle lispeth,

The slumbrous wave outwelleth,

The babbling runnel crispeth,

The hollow grot replieth

Where Claribel low-lieth.

Crossing the Bar

Sunset and evening star,
    And one clear call for me!
And may there be no moaning of the bar,
    When I put out to sea,

    But such a tide as moving seems asleep,
    Too full for sound and foam,
When that which drew from out the boundless deep
    Turns again home.

    Twilight and evening bell,
    And after that the dark!
And may there be no sadness of farewell,
    When I embark;

    For tho' from out our bourne of Time and Place
    The flood may bear me far,
I hope to see my Pilot face to face

When I have crost the bar.

The Eagle

He clasps the crag with crooked hands;
Close to the sun in lonely lands,
Ring'd with the azure world, he stands.

The wrinkled sea beneath him crawls;
He watches from his mountain walls,
And like a thunderbolt he falls.

The Higher Pantheism

The sun, the moon, the stars, the seas, the hills and the plains,-

Are not these, O Soul, the Vision of Him who reigns?

Is not the Vision He, tho' He be not that which He seems?

Dreams are true while they last, and do we not live in dreams?

Earth, these solid stars, this weight of body and limb,

Are they not sign and symbol of thy division from Him?

Dark is the world to thee; thyself art the reason why,

For is He not all but thou, that hast power to feel "I am I"?

Glory about thee, without thee; and thou fulfillest thy doom,

Making Him broken gleams and a stifled splendour and gloom.

Speak to Him, thou, for He hears, and Spirit with Spirit can meet-

Closer is He than breathing, and nearer than hands and feet.

God is law, say the wise; O soul, and let us rejoice,

For if He thunder by law the thunder is yet His voice.

Law is God, say some; no God at all, says the fool,

For all we have power to see is a straight staff bent in a pool;

And the ear of man cannot hear, and the eye of man cannot see;

But if we could see and hear, this Vision-were it not He?

MLA Style Citations for Scholarly Secondary Sources, Peer-Reviewed Journal Articles and Critical Academic Research Essays

"Charge of the Light Brigade, The." *Merriam Webster's*

Encyclopedia of Literature, Merriam-Webster,

1995. *Something About The Author Online*,

http://link.galegroup.com/apps/doc/A148916164/GLS?u=fjp

_jvpl&sid=GLS&xid=a74370ab.

"Early Plays and Idylls." *British Writers, Supplement 16*, edited by

Jay Parini, Charles Scribner's Sons, 2010, pp. 3-9. *Scribner*

Writer Series,

http://link.galegroup.com/apps/doc/CX2356300013/GLS?u=f

jp_jvpl&sid=GLS&xid=13182d57.

"The Audience and Nineteenth-Century Literature." *Nineteenth-*

Century Literature Criticism, edited by Jessica Bomarito and

Russel Whitaker, vol. 160, Gale, 2006. *Literature Resource*

Center,

http://link.galegroup.com/apps/doc/H1410001520/GLS?u=fj

p_jvpl&sid=GLS&xid=b7eff608.

"The Railroad in Nineteenth-Century Literature." *Nineteenth-*

Century Literature Criticism, edited by Kathy D. Darrow and

Russel Whitaker, vol. 184, Gale, 2007. *Literature Resource*

Center,

http://link.galegroup.com/apps/doc/H1410001877/GLS?u=fj

p_jvpl&sid=GLS&xid=8fd3e083.

Blandford, Roger D. "The charge of the light brigade." *Nature*

377.6549 (1995): 477-478.

Bowles, Noelle. "Tennyson's Idylls of the King and Anglican

Authority." *Nineteenth-Century Literature Criticism*, edited

by Kathy D. Darrow, vol. 202, Gale, 2009. *Literature*

Criticism Online,

http://link.galegroup.com/apps/doc/RHSLOF804074063/GL

S?u=fjp_jvpl&sid=GLS&xid=c915a33c. Originally

published in *Christianity and Literature*, vol. 56, no. 4,

Summer 2007, pp. 573-594.

Bowles, Noelle. "Tennyson's *Idylls of the King* and Anglican

Authority." *Poetry Criticism*, edited by Michelle Lee, vol.

101, Gale, 2010. *Literature Resource Center*, http://link.galegroup.com/apps/doc/H1420094575/GLS?u=fj p_jvpl&sid=GLS&xid=99c2cd63. Originally published in *Christianity and Literature*, vol. 56, no. 4, Summer 2007, pp. 573-594.

Butler, Lance St. John. "In Memoriam: Overview." *Reference Guide to English Literature*, edited by D. L. Kirkpatrick, 2nd ed., St. James Press, 1991. *Literature Resource Center*, http://link.galegroup.com/apps/doc/H1420007896/GLS?u=fj p_jvpl&sid=GLS&xid=361a2234.

Camlot, Jason. "The Charge of the Light Brigade." *Victorian Review* 35.1 (2009): 27-32.

Clemons, Walter. "Volley and Thunder." *Contemporary Literary Criticism*, edited by Carolyn Riley and Phyllis Carmel Mendelson, vol. 6, Gale, 1976. *Literature Criticism Online*, http://link.galegroup.com/apps/doc/WIJNLC302936550/GLS ?u=fjp_jvpl&sid=GLS&xid=c0d6a076. Originally published in *Newsweek*, 21 Oct. 1974, p. 110.

Cronin, Richard. "Edward Lear and Tennyson's

Nonsense." *Children's Literature Review*, edited by Jelena

Krstovic, vol. 169, Gale, 2012. *Literature Criticism Online*,

http://link.galegroup.com/apps/doc/OGLCJB173212067/GLS

?u=fjp_jvpl&sid=GLS&xid=bf572176. Originally published

in *Tennyson Among the Poets: Bicentenary Essays*, edited by

Robert Douglas-Fairhurst and Seamus Perry, Oxford

University Press, Inc., 2009, pp. 259-275.

Evans, Lloyd. "Melody maker: Lloyd Evans celebrates Tennyson's

miraculous musicality." *Spectator*, 1 Aug. 2009, p.

29+. *Literature Resource Center*,

http://link.galegroup.com/apps/doc/A204861944/GLS?u=fjp

_jvpl&sid=GLS&xid=6e276902.

Fisher, Devon. "In Graceful Service to the Queen (Bee): The

Politics of the Hive in Tennyson's *The Princess*." *Nineteenth-

Century Literature Criticism*, edited by Kathy D. Darrow,

vol. 202, Gale, 2009. *Literature Resource Center*,

http://link.galegroup.com/apps/doc/H1420086159/GLS?u=fj

p_jvpl&sid=GLS&xid=f42154ca. Originally published in *Victorians Institute Journal*, vol. 32, 2004, pp. 107-128.

Foltinek, Herbert. "Their's Not to Reason Why: Alfred Lord Tennyson on the Human Condition." *Nineteenth-Century Literature Criticism*, edited by Laurie DiMauro, vol. 30, Gale, 1991. *Literature Criticism Online*, http://link.galegroup.com/apps/doc/DUSBIO893697003/GLS ?u=fjp_jvpl&sid=GLS&xid=76914a48. Originally published in *A Yearbook of Studies in English Language and Literature*, vol. 80, 1985, pp. 27-38.

Gallagher, John. "A Unique and Haunting Vision of Wartime Chaos and Death." *Contemporary Literary Criticism*, edited by Jeffrey W. Hunter, vol. 130, Gale, 2000. *Literature Resource Center*, http://link.galegroup.com/apps/doc/H1100031696/GLS?u=fj p_jvpl&sid=GLS&xid=4790a3e1. Originally published in *Chicago Tribune*, 7 Dec. 1998, p. 3.

Hack, Daniel. "Wild charges: the Afro-Haitian 'charge of the light brigade'." *Victorian Studies*, vol. 54, no. 2, 2012, p. 199+. *Literature Resource Center*, http://link.galegroup.com/apps/doc/A293949955/GLS?u=fjp _jvpl&sid=GLS&xid=a6472b75.

Hughes, John. "'Hang there like fruit, my soul': Tennyson's feminine imaginings." *Victorian Poetry*, vol. 45, no. 2, 2007, p. 95+. *Literature Resource Center*, http://link.galegroup.com/apps/doc/A167430457/GLS?u=fjp _jvpl&sid=GLS&xid=39095b04.

Hughes, Linda K. "Tennyson." *Victorian Poetry*, vol. 42, no. 3, 2004, p. 409+. *Literature Resource Center*, http://link.galegroup.com/apps/doc/A126357142/GLS?u=fjp _jvpl&sid=GLS&xid=25bac35c.

Jackson, Martin A. "The Charge of the Light Brigade." *Film & History: An Interdisciplinary Journal of Film and Television Studies* 2.3 (1973): 20-21.

Kelly, David. "Critical Essay on 'The Eagle'." *Poetry for Students*,

    edited by Elizabeth Thomason, vol. 11, Gale,

    2001. *Literature Resource Center*,

    http://link.galegroup.com/apps/doc/H1420035658/GLS?u=fj

    p_jvpl&sid=GLS&xid=e2405813.

Markley, Arnold. "An overview of "The Charge of the Light

    Brigade"." *Poetry for Students*, Gale. *Literature Resource*

    Center,

    http://link.galegroup.com/apps/doc/H1420001551/GLS?u=fj

    p_jvpl&sid=GLS&xid=b7aff64a.

Markovits, Stefanie. "Giving voice to the Crimean War: Tennyson's

    'charge' and Maud's battle-song." *Victorian Poetry*, vol. 47,

    no. 3, 2009, p. 481+. *Literature Resource Center*,

    http://link.galegroup.com/apps/doc/A213777318/GLS?u=fjp

    _jvpl&sid=GLS&xid=96948c35.

Morton, John. "Tennyson and the 1914-1918 War." *Poetry*

    Criticism, edited by Michelle Lee, vol. 101, Gale,

    2010. *Literature Resource Center*,

http://link.galegroup.com/apps/doc/H1420094573/GLS?u=fj
p_jvpl&sid=GLS&xid=8aa9fc6a. Originally published
in *Tennyson Research Bulletin*, vol. 8, no. 5, Nov. 2006, pp.
353-367.

Perry, Seamus. "Returns." *Poetry Criticism*, edited by Michelle Lee,
vol. 101, Gale, 2010. *Literature Resource Center*,
http://link.galegroup.com/apps/doc/H1420094571/GLS?u=fj
p_jvpl&sid=GLS&xid=9f6a487a. Originally published
in *Alfred Tennyson*, . Horndon, United Kingdom: Northcote,
2005, pp. 19-56.

Purton, Valerie. "Tennyson, Heidegger, and the problematics of
'home'." *Victorian Poetry*, vol. 50, no. 2, 2012, p.
227+. *Literature Resource Center*,
http://link.galegroup.com/apps/doc/A294895608/GLS?u=fjp
_jvpl&sid=GLS&xid=36eb7eb7.

Renk, Kathleen Williams. ""Debating Darwin: The Alchemy of A.
S. Byatt and Pauline Melville"." *Contemporary Literary
Criticism*, edited by Lawrence J. Trudeau, vol. 385, Gale,

2016. *Literature Resource Center,*

http://link.galegroup.com/apps/doc/H1100120191/GLS?u=fj

p_jvpl&sid=GLS&xid=de93c8d4.

Robisch, S. K. "Critical Essay on 'The Eagle'." *Poetry for Students,*

edited by Elizabeth Thomason, vol. 11, Gale,

2001. *Literature Resource Center,*

http://link.galegroup.com/apps/doc/H1420035659/GLS?u=fj

p_jvpl&sid=GLS&xid=4d401b1c.

Saintsbury, George. "Tennyson' and 'Tennyson." *Nineteenth-*

Century Literature Criticism, edited by Laurie DiMauro, vol.

30, Gale, 1991. *Literature Resource Center,*

http://link.galegroup.com/apps/doc/H1420020374/GLS?u=fj

p_jvpl&sid=GLS&xid=fb4ebc63. Originally published

in *Corrected Impressions: Essays on Victorian Writers,* by

George Saintsbury, Dodd, Mead and Company, 1895, pp. 21-

30.

Shaw, W. David. "Poems that Disturb or Transform Their

Genres." *Alfred Lord Tennyson: The Poet in an Age of*

Theory, Twayne Publishers, 1996, pp. 25-35. Twayne's

English Authors Series 525. *Twayne's Authors Series*,

http://link.galegroup.com/apps/doc/CX2459300012/GLS?u=f

jp_jvpl&sid=GLS&xid=d4aa98c4.

Small, Helen. "Tennyson and Late Style." *Nineteenth-Century*

Literature Criticism, edited by Kathy D. Darrow, vol. 202,

Gale, 2009. *Literature Resource Center*,

http://link.galegroup.com/apps/doc/H1420086161/GLS?u=fj

p_jvpl&sid=GLS&xid=d8ff9698. Originally published

in *Tennyson Research Bulletin*, vol. 8, no. 4, Nov. 2005, pp.

226-250.

Taaffe, James G. "Circle Imagery in Tennyson's in

Memoriam." *Nineteenth-Century Literature Criticism*, edited

by Lynn M. Zott, vol. 115, Gale, 2003. *Literature Criticism*

Online,

http://link.galegroup.com/apps/doc/HVRQUF194671210/GL

S?u=fjp_jvpl&sid=GLS&xid=6b888e98. Originally

published in *Victorian Poetry*, vol. 1, no. 2, Apr. 1963, pp.

123-131.

Watts, Nevile Hunter. "The Englishness of English
    Literature." *Vision Splendid*, by Nevile Watts, Sheed And
    Ward, 1946, p. 109. *LitFinder*,
    http://link.galegroup.com/apps/doc/LTF0000754361WK/GL
    S?u=fjp_jvpl&sid=GLS&xid=b6e6dcb4.

Woodcock, George. "The Rival Bards: Alice Munro's Lives of Girls
    and Women & Victorian Poetry." *Contemporary Literary
    Criticism*, edited by Jeffrey W. Hunter, vol. 222, Gale,
    2006. *Literature Criticism Online*,
    http://link.galegroup.com/apps/doc/SPMDTD651759775/GL
    S?u=fjp_jvpl&sid=GLS&xid=5d6cba34. Originally
    published in *Canadian Literature*, Spring 1987, pp. 211-216.

Worth, Aaron. "Tennyson and the poetics of alterity." *Victorian
    Newsletter*, vol. 117, 2010, p. 75+. *Literature Resource
    Center*,
    http://link.galegroup.com/apps/doc/A230765401/GLS?u=fjp
    _jvpl&sid=GLS&xid=749707a9.

Printed in Great Britain
by Amazon

56709775R00023